35 STEPS TO MAKE YOUR PET INTERNET FAMOUS

The Pet Influencer Handbook

Melody Satin

Hey there, fellow pet enthusiast! Ready to turn your pet into the next internet sensation? If by the end, your furry (or scaly, or feathery) friend is on the path to internet stardom, could you take a minute to leave a review? It'll mean the world to me and might just inspire the next pet influencer out there. Cheers to our pets taking over the internet!

PROLOGUE

In the age of the internet, where viral sensations are born overnight and memes become the language of the masses, a new kind of star has emerged: the pet influencer. From cats that play the piano to dogs with impeccable fashion sense, our four-legged (and sometimes feathered or finned) friends have taken the digital world by storm.

But behind every pet that's a sensation, there's an owner with a vision, a strategy, and a lot of love. Making your pet internet famous isn't just about capturing a quirky moment on camera—it's about understanding the digital landscape, building a brand, and most importantly, ensuring the well-being and happiness of your beloved companion.

You might be wondering: Why would anyone want to make their pet internet famous? The reasons are as varied as the pets themselves. For some, it's the allure of connecting with a global community of pet lovers. For others, it's the potential for brand collaborations or even a new career path. But at its heart, it's about celebrating the joy, laughter, and unconditional love that pets bring into our lives.

This handbook is your roadmap to navigating the world of pet influencing. Whether you're just starting out or looking to take your pet's online presence to the next level, the steps outlined in these pages will guide you on a journey filled with fun, challenges, and countless rewards.

So, are you ready to embark on this adventure? Your pet might just be the next big internet sensation, and together, you can share your story with the world.

CHAPTER 1: LAYING THE GROUNDWORK

"Every pet has a story. It's up to you to share it with the world."

Before your pet can become the next internet sensation, there are foundational steps you need to take. This chapter will guide you through understanding your pet's unique personality, setting realistic expectations, and the ethics of pet influencer culture.

1. Understanding Your Pet's Personality

"Every whisker twitch, tail wag, and chirp tells a story."

The Tapestry of Temperaments

Just as humans have varied personalities, pets too come with their own set of quirks, preferences, and temperaments. Recognizing and celebrating these individual traits not only strengthens your bond with your pet but also provides a goldmine of content opportunities.

Examples of Unique Pet Personalities:

1. The Adventurous Climber: Mr. Whiskers, a domestic cat, might not be satisfied with just lounging around. Instead, he could have an adventurous streak, scaling tall bookshelves or perching on top of doors. Content showcasing his climbing antics could be both entertaining and relatable to other cat owners.

2. The Melodious Critic: Perhaps Bella, your parrot, has a habit of chirping or squawking along to specific genres of music but stays silent or even shows displeasure for others. Recording her reactions to different tunes can be both hilarious and endearing.

3. The Pensive Pooch: While most dogs might be known for their boundless energy, your dog, Buddy, might be the contemplative type. He could spend hours just gazing out of the window, lost in thought. Capturing these serene moments can offer a calming and different perspective to dog content.

4. The Foodie Tortoise: Tortoises are generally not associated with being picky eaters. But imagine if your tortoise, Sheldon, shows a clear preference for certain veggies over others, or even does a little 'happy dance' when presented with his favorite treat. Documenting Sheldon's culinary adventures can be both educational and delightful.

5. The Social Butterfly: Goldfish are often seen as simple pets with not much personality. But what if your goldfish, Goldie, always swims excitedly to the front of the tank whenever someone approaches? Or perhaps she has a particular routine with her tank mates? Highlighting these social interactions can debunk myths about fish and showcase their personalities.

Action Step: Spend a week jotting down notes about your pet's behavior, habits, and reactions to different situations. Set up a camera or your phone to record during times you're not actively observing. Often, pets showcase their quirkiest behaviors when they believe no one is watching. Reviewing this footage can give you insights into their unique personality and provide content ideas.

Understanding and showcasing your pet's personality not only provides authentic content but also helps in building a genuine connection with your audience. After all, it's these individual quirks and habits that make our pets so endearing and memorable.

2. Setting Realistic Expectations

"Every journey begins with a single paw step."

The Reality of the Digital Landscape

The digital world, while brimming with opportunities, is also saturated with content. The allure of instant virality can sometimes overshadow the consistent effort and patience required to genuinely connect with an audience. By setting realistic expectations, you not only set yourself up for sustainable growth but also ensure the journey remains enjoyable and stress-free for both you and your pet.

Examples of Realistic Expectations:

1. The Slow Burn: Imagine you've started an Instagram account for your hedgehog. In the first month, despite regular posts, you only gain 50 followers. Instead of feeling disheartened, remember that these are 50 individuals genuinely interested in Spike's adventures. Quality often trumps quantity.

2. Engagement Over Numbers: Your rabbit, Fluffy, might have 200 followers on TikTok, but each video gets numerous comments and shares. Instead of focusing on the follower count, celebrate the high engagement. Engaged followers are more likely to share, comment, and interact, leading to organic growth.

3. Learning Curve: Perhaps you've started a YouTube channel for your pet snake. The first few videos might not be perfect, with lighting issues or shaky camera work. Instead of aiming for perfection, set the expectation of improvement. With each video, you'll learn and refine your skills.

4. Brand Collaborations: After a few months of consistent posting, a small pet toy brand reaches out for a collaboration with your dog. While it might not be a high-end brand or a paid collaboration, it's a start. Setting the expectation of starting small and gradually moving to bigger brands can be more realistic and fulfilling.

5. Content Creation: While some pet influencers post daily, it might not be feasible for everyone, especially if you're juggling other responsibilities. Instead of aiming for daily posts, set a realistic goal of 3 quality posts a week for your cat's Facebook page.

Action Step: Create a vision board or a digital spreadsheet for your pet's online journey. Break down your overarching goals into monthly or even weekly objectives. This could include targets for follower growth, engagement rates, content creation, skill development (like photography or video editing), and networking or collaboration efforts. Regularly review and adjust these goals based on your progress and learnings.

Setting realistic expectations doesn't mean limiting your ambitions. Instead, it's about understanding the journey's nature, celebrating every step, and ensuring that the process is as enjoyable and rewarding as the milestones you're aiming for.

3. The Ethics of Pet Influencer Culture

"In the spotlight of fame, the well-being of our furry, feathered, or scaled companions must always shine the brightest."

Navigating the Thin Line

The digital age has brought about countless opportunities for pets to charm audiences worldwide. However, with this newfound fame comes the responsibility of ensuring that our pets are treated with love, respect, and care. The line between entertaining content and exploitation can sometimes be thin, and it's essential to navigate this space ethically.

Examples of Ethical Considerations:

1. Costume Concerns: Dressing up pets can be adorable and a significant trend in pet content. However, if your bird, Tweetie, shows signs of distress or discomfort in a costume, it's essential to prioritize her comfort over content. Some pets might feel restricted or scared in outfits, while others might enjoy them. Always observe and respect their reactions.

2. Trick or Trauma: Training pets to do tricks can be entertaining, but forcing them into unnatural or uncomfortable positions can be harmful. For instance, if your cat doesn't naturally stand on his hind legs, pushing him to do so repeatedly for a video can cause distress or even injury.

3. Product Partnerships: When approached by a brand for a collaboration, it's tempting to say yes, especially if there's a lucrative offer on the table. However, if a dog treat brand has ingredients that you wouldn't give your dog, it's essential to decline the offer, regardless of the potential monetary gain.

4. Environment and Setting: If your fish lives in a specific water temperature and environment, moving him to a different tank for a "better-looking" backdrop can be stressful and harmful. Always ensure that the settings for shoots or content creation are safe and comfortable for your pet.

5. Frequency of Filming: While your rabbit, might be okay with a 5-minute filming session, extending it to an hour can be exhausting and stressful for him. It's crucial to limit the duration of shoots and give your pets ample breaks.

Action Step: Dedicate a day to sit down and reflect on your pet's personality, likes, dislikes, and comfort levels. Based on this, create a list of "non-negotiables" for your pet's online presence. This list can include:

- No costumes or outfits that cause distress or discomfort.

- No collaborations with brands that don't align with your pet's well-being.

- Limiting filming or photo sessions to a specific duration.

- Avoiding certain environments or settings that might be stressful or harmful.

- No forceful actions or tricks that go against the pet's natural behavior.

Ethics in pet influencer culture isn't just about avoiding harm; it's about actively ensuring that every decision made prioritizes the pet's well-being. In the end, the genuine love and care you show your pet will resonate more with audiences than any forced trick or trend.

4. Creating a Unique Brand for Your Pet

"In the vast digital jungle, let your pet's unique roar, chirp, or meow stand out."

The Essence of Branding

Branding isn't just about logos or color schemes; it's about creating a distinct identity that captures the essence of your pet. This identity should be consistent, memorable, and, most importantly, genuine. When done right, it can set your pet apart in a saturated online space and create a loyal community of followers.

Examples of Unique Branding Ideas:

1. The Vintage Vibe: Let's say your cat has a regal demeanor and loves lounging on vintage furniture in your home. Her brand could revolve around a vintage aesthetic, with sepia-toned photos, classical music in videos, and captions that reflect old-world charm.

2. #SunnySundays: Perhaps your dog, Sunny, is most active and playful on Sundays. You could create a recurring hashtag,

#SunnySundays, where every Sunday, you post content of Sunny indulging in his favorite activities, creating anticipation among your followers.

3. The Bowtie Bunny: If your rabbit, Mr. Hops, looks adorable and doesn't mind wearing a bowtie, it could become his signature look. Every piece of content could feature him in different colored or patterned bowties, making him instantly recognizable.

4. Travel Tales with Tina: Suppose your pet bird, Tina, often travels with you, whether it's a trip to the local park or a vacation. Her brand could revolve around these adventures, showcasing her experiences in different places, complete with a travel diary or map tracking her journeys.

5. Chef Whisker's Delights: Imagine your cat, Whiskers, has a curious palate and often sniffs or "tastes" various (safe) foods. You could create content around "Whisker's Food Reviews," where he "rates" different foods based on his reactions, complete with a chef's hat and playful commentary.

Action Step: Dedicate a quiet afternoon to reflect on your pet's personality, habits, and quirks. Based on these reflections, brainstorm five potential branding ideas:

1. Color Scheme: Perhaps a pastel theme for a calm and serene pet or vibrant colors for an energetic one.

2. Content Type: This could range from adventure vlogs, DIY toy sessions, or even "day in the life" videos.

3. Signature Accessory: Something your pet is comfortable wearing, like a specific collar, hat, or bandana.

4. Catchphrase: A fun phrase that captures your pet's essence, like "Paws and Reflect" for a contemplative cat or "Flying High" for an energetic bird.

5. Recurring Hashtag: A weekly or monthly content theme that followers can look forward to, like #MuddyMondays for a dog who loves to play in the mud.

Creating a unique brand for your pet is about celebrating their individuality and presenting it in a way that's both engaging and authentic. It's this authenticity, combined with a distinct identity, that will make your pet a memorable figure in the vast world of pet influencers.

5. Setting Up Dedicated Social Media Profiles

"Crafting a digital den where your pet's personality shines."

The Importance of Separate Spaces

While it might be tempting to share your pet's antics on your personal profile, having a dedicated space for them offers numerous advantages. It provides clarity for your audience, allows for focused content strategies, and can even open up monetization and collaboration opportunities that might not be suitable for personal profiles.

Examples of Setting Up and Curating Dedicated Profiles:

1. The Instagram Starlet: Let's say your dog, Daisy, has a penchant for striking dramatic poses. Instagram, with its visual focus, would be an ideal platform. Her profile, "@DramaticDaisy," could feature high-quality photos, behind-the-scenes stories, and even IGTV videos of her "modeling sessions."

2. TikTok Dancer: Perhaps your parrot, Pedro, loves bobbing his head to music beats. A TikTok profile, "@PedroTheGroover," could showcase short, engaging clips of Pedro dancing to popular tracks, remixes, or even original compositions.

3. YouTube Adventurer: If your cat, Cleo, is an explorer, always curious and getting into amusing situations, a YouTube channel named "Cleo's Chronicles" could feature longer videos of her adventures, from exploring new toys to her reactions to different stimuli.

4. Twitter Commentator: Imagine your bunny, Benny, has a lot of "opinions" on various matters, from the brand of his food to the state of the garden. A Twitter profile, "@BennySpeaks," could be a humorous take on his "thoughts," giving him a witty, sassy online voice.

5. Pinterest Fashionista: Your reptile, Remy, might have a collection of adorable outfits or accessories. A Pinterest board, "Remy's Runway," could curate photos of him donning different looks, along with links to buy similar items or DIY outfit tutorials.

Action Step:

1. Platform Selection: Based on your pet's personality and the type of content you envision, choose one or two platforms to start. For visually appealing content, Instagram or Pinterest might be ideal. For more dynamic or video content, TikTok or YouTube could be more suitable.

*2. Profile Creation: U*se your pet's name or a catchy username that's easy to remember and search for. Ensure the username aligns with your pet's brand and personality.

3. Bio Crafting: Write a concise, engaging bio that gives new visitors an idea of what to expect. For instance, "@DramaticDaisy: Striking a pose, one day at a time. #ModelPup"

4. Content Strategy: Before you start posting, plan out the first few weeks of content. This ensures consistency and gives you time to gauge audience reactions and adjust accordingly.

Dedicated social media profiles not only professionalize your pet's online presence but also offer a space where their personality can shine unabated. As you curate this space, always prioritize authenticity, ensuring that every post, story, or tweet genuinely reflects your pet's unique charm.

CHAPTER 2: CONTENT CREATION

"Content is king, but character is the crown."

Creating compelling content is at the heart of any successful online presence. For your pet, this means capturing moments that resonate with viewers, evoke emotions, and showcase their unique personality. This chapter will guide you through finding your pet's niche, mastering pet photography, and crafting engaging videos and captions.

6. Finding Your Pet's "Angle" or "Niche"

"In a digital world filled with paws and whiskers, let your pet's unique quirk be their signature."

The Power of Specialization

While the internet loves pets in general, having a specific theme or niche can make your pet stand out. This specialization not only helps in creating a distinct brand identity but also attracts a more engaged and loyal audience who share an interest in that particular niche.

Examples of Unique Pet Niches:

1. The Literary Feline: Imagine your cat, Muffin, often curls up beside you when you read. She seems to have a penchant for lounging on open books or playfully batting at bookmarks. Her niche could be "books and literature." Her profile, "@LiteraryMuffin," could feature photos of her with different books, playful "reviews" of books based on how much she enjoyed sitting on them, and even recommendations for cozy reading nooks.

2. The Gardening Guinea Pig: Your guinea pig, Gigi, might love spending time in your garden, nibbling on fresh greens and exploring flower beds. Her niche could revolve around gardening. Posts could showcase her adventures among the plants, tips on pet-safe plants, and even "helping" you with gardening chores.

3. The DIY Dog: If your dog, Duke, gets excited every time you bring out the craft supplies and loves playing with homemade toys, a DIY niche might be perfect. Content could include tutorials on making pet-friendly toys, Duke "assisting" in craft projects, and reviews of his favorite DIY creations.

4. The Yoga Bunny: Perhaps your rabbit, Rumi, often strikes poses that uncannily resemble yoga asanas. This could lead to a niche centered around "bunny yoga." Videos could showcase Rumi "practicing" her stretches, paired with calming music and playful commentary on the benefits of each "asana."

5. The Gourmet Gecko: Your gecko, Gordon, has a refined palate, showing clear preferences for certain foods. His niche could be "fine dining" or "food reviews." Content could feature Gordon "tasting" different foods, with humorous ratings and even "cooking" sessions where he "prepares" his meals.

Action Step:

1. Observation: Spend a few days closely observing your pet. Note down any unique behaviors, preferences, or quirks they exhibit.

2. Research: Look up popular pet influencers and see if there's an untapped niche that your pet naturally fits into.

3. List Creation: Based on your observations and research, list down three potential niches. For instance:

- Artistic Angle: If your pet shows interest in paints (non-toxic) or art supplies, they could "create" art pieces.

- Music Maestro: If your pet reacts amusingly to different music genres, content could revolve around their "musical critiques."

- Adventure Enthusiast: If your pet loves exploring new environments, their niche could be centered around their adventures, be it in nature or urban settings.

Finding a niche for your pet is about amplifying their natural behaviors and interests in a fun, engaging manner. It not only provides direction for content creation but also helps in building a community of followers who share a love for that specific theme.

7. Investing in a Good Camera

"In the world of pixels and posts, clarity is king."

The Visual Advantage

In the realm of social media, where users often scroll rapidly through their feeds, a crisp, clear, and well-composed photo can make someone stop and engage. While the subject (your pet) remains the star, the quality of the image can significantly enhance the storytelling.

Examples of Camera Benefits:

1. Depth of Field: A dedicated camera, especially one with interchangeable lenses, can give you a beautiful depth of field, where your pet is in sharp focus while the background is softly blurred. Imagine a photo of your cat, Luna, with her eyes sharply in focus, while the background fades into a dreamy blur, making her gaze even more captivating.

2. Low-Light Performance: Pets, especially cats, can be most active during dawn or dusk. A camera with good low-light performance can capture these moments without the graininess or noise that many smartphones produce. Picture your dog, Max, playing fetch as the sun sets, the golden hues captured perfectly without any loss of detail.

3. Fast Autofocus: Pets are unpredictable. One moment they're sitting still, and the next, they're darting across the room. A camera with fast autofocus ensures you capture those spontaneous moments in sharp clarity, like your bird, Kiwi, suddenly taking flight.

4. Zoom Capabilities: If you're in a park or a larger space, a camera with optical zoom can help you capture close-ups of your pet without physically moving closer, ensuring you don't miss moments like your rabbit, Thumper, interacting with other animals from a distance.

5. Versatility: With a dedicated camera, you have the flexibility to change settings, lenses, and modes based on the situation. This versatility can be especially useful for capturing diverse content, from slow-motion videos of your fish, Bubbles, swimming to time-lapses of your tortoise, Sheldon, exploring the garden.

Action Step:

1. Budgeting: Determine a budget for your camera investment. Remember, sometimes spending a bit more upfront can save costs in the long run due to better durability and performance.

2. Research: Look up reviews and comparisons online. Websites like DPReview or Camera Labs offer in-depth analyses of cameras, often with a focus on specific features.

3. Key Features: Prioritize features that cater to pet photography. As mentioned, good low-light performance, fast autofocus, and optical zoom can be particularly beneficial.

4. Test Before Buying: If possible, visit a camera store and test a few models. See how they feel in your hand, check the ease of use, and even bring a few sample shots of your pet to see how the camera captures them.

5. Consider Second-Hand: Sometimes, a well-maintained second-hand camera can offer excellent value for money. Platforms like KEH or even local camera groups can be good places to explore.

Investing in a good camera is not just about better image quality; it's about ensuring that the moments you capture of your pet are as vivid, clear, and memorable as the real-life experiences.

8. The Basics of Pet Photography

"Capturing the essence of whiskers, wags, and wings in a frame."

The Art of Pet Portraiture

While pets are naturally photogenic, capturing their essence requires a blend of patience, technique, and understanding of their behavior. Mastering the basics of pet photography ensures that you not only get Instagram-worthy shots but also create lasting memories of your furry, feathered, or scaled companion.

Examples and Tips for Pet Photography:

1. Golden Hour Glow: The hour just after sunrise and before sunset, often referred to as the 'golden hour,' provides soft, warm lighting. Imagine capturing your dog, Bella, during this time, her fur illuminated with a golden hue, adding a magical touch to the photo.

2. Pet's Perspective: Getting down to your pet's level offers a unique perspective and makes the photo more immersive. A ground-level shot of your cat, Whiskers, can showcase the world from his viewpoint, making the viewer feel like they're right there with him.

3. Engagement Tools: Using toys or treats not only grabs their attention but can also evoke playful or curious expressions. Picture your parrot, Polly, tilting her head curiously at a shiny bell, or your rabbit, Mopsy, standing on her hind legs, reaching for a treat.

4. Candid Over Posed: While posed shots are great, candid moments often capture the true essence of your pet. A candid shot of your fish, Fin, suddenly darting around when a new plant is introduced, or your lizard, Leo, lazily stretching after a nap, can be heartwarming and genuine.

5. Focus on the Eyes: A pet's eyes are often expressive. Ensuring they're in focus can make a photo more impactful. The gleam in your dog, Rover's eyes as he waits for a ball to be thrown, or the gentle gaze of your cat, Misty, as she lounges can convey a myriad of emotions.

6. Patience is Key: Pets are unpredictable. Sometimes, the best shots come after waiting patiently for the right moment. It could be waiting for your turtle, Toto, to peek out of his shell or for your hamster, Hubble, to pause atop his wheel.

Action Step:

1. Scout Locations: Before the photography session, look around your home or nearby parks for spots with good lighting and minimal distractions.

2. Equipment Check: Ensure your camera or smartphone is charged, and clear out memory space. If you have them, bring along props, toys, or treats.

3. Practice Session: Dedicate a day to pet photography. Start with posed shots to get your pet acclimated to the camera. Then, as they relax, capture candid moments.

4. Experiment: Play with different angles, get close for detailed shots, or pull back for environmental portraits. Try different settings on your camera, like portrait mode or macro, to see what enhances your shots.

5. Review and Learn: At the end of the session, review your photos. Note what worked and what didn't. Over time, you'll develop a better understanding of your pet's angles and the techniques that capture them best.

Mastering pet photography is a journey of understanding your pet's personality and merging it with technical know-how. With each click, you're not just taking a photo but capturing a moment, a memory, a piece of the bond you share with your pet.

9. Video Essentials: From Cute Antics to Tutorials

"In the cinema of cuteness, every wag, chirp, and purr is a blockbuster."

The Dynamic World of Pet Videos

While photos capture a moment, videos capture the essence of time, showcasing the range of your pet's behaviors, sounds, and interactions. With the rise of platforms like TikTok and Instagram Reels, video content has become a dominant force in the pet influencer sphere.

Examples and Tips for Pet Video Creation:

1. Bite-Sized Cuteness: For platforms like TikTok or Instagram Reels, short, engaging clips work best. Imagine capturing your cat, Purrlock, in a 15-second video, slowly stalking a toy, only to hilariously lose interest at the last second.

2. Tutorial Time: If your dog, Barkley, has mastered a new trick, a tutorial video can be both educational and entertaining. Start with a teaser of the final trick, then break down the steps, showcasing Barkley's progress and reactions.

3. Storytelling: Create a narrative around your pet's activities. Perhaps your bird, Chirpy, has a "morning routine" of singing, preening, and playing. A video that follows this routine, complete with playful commentary, can be a hit.

4. Quality Matters: Ensure videos are well-lit. Natural light works best, but if filming indoors, use lamps or lights to eliminate shadows. A clear audio, free from background noises, enhances the viewer's experience.

5. Editing Magic: Use apps like InShot, Adobe Premiere Rush, or iMovie to edit your videos. Add captions to provide context, use music to set the mood, and include effects or transitions to make the video more engaging. For instance, a slow-motion effect of your hamster, Wheelie, taking a leap or a time-lapse of your turtle, Slowpoke, exploring the garden can add a unique touch.

Action Step:

1. Plan Ahead: Before hitting the record button, have a rough idea of what you want to capture. Whether it's a candid moment or a structured tutorial, planning ensures smoother filming.

2. Film More, Use Less: It's always better to have more footage than you need. This gives you flexibility during editing and ensures you don't miss any cute or crucial moments.

3. Experiment with Angles: Try filming from different perspectives. A ground-level shot of your rabbit, Hopster, can be more immersive, while an overhead shot of your fish, Glitter, showcases her patterns and tank layout.

4. Editing Session: Once you've captured your footage, spend time editing. Trim unnecessary parts, add music or voiceovers, and play with effects to enhance the video's appeal.

5. Feedback Loop: Before posting, show the video to friends or family. Their feedback can provide insights into any changes needed or confirm that it's ready to charm the online world.

Videos offer a dynamic way to share your pet's world with the audience. With the right mix of content, quality, and editing, each video becomes a mini-movie, with your pet as the star, ready to captivate hearts and screens worldwide.

10. The Art of the Caption

Captions provide context, evoke emotions, and invite engagement. Especially for pet influencers, captions become the voice that narrates their stories and shares their thoughts.

Examples and Tips for Crafting Captions:

1. Humor and Wit: For a photo of a cat sprawled out lazily in a sunbeam, a caption like, "Channeling my inner sun goddess. ☀️□ #LazySunday" adds a touch of humor.

2. Heartfelt Moments: For a video where a dog is patiently waiting by the door, a caption like, "Every minute feels like an hour when we're apart. ❤️□" can tug at the heartstrings.

3. Narrative from Their Perspective: Imagine a bird looking curiously at the camera. A caption like, "Why do you always point that strange device at me?" gives a playful voice to the pet.

4. Engagement Invites: For a picture surrounded by toys, a caption like, "Having a hard time picking today's toy. Which one's your favorite?" invites comments and interactions.

5. Educational or Informative: If you've posted a tutorial of teaching a parrot a new word, a caption like, "Did you know parrots mimic sounds to bond with their flock?" educates while showcasing the content.

Action Step:

1. Visual Analysis: Look at the photo or video. What's the primary emotion or theme it conveys?

2. Tone Setting: Decide on the tone you want for the caption. Humorous, reflective, educational, or conversational?

3. Drafting: For a picture of a fish blowing bubbles, consider:

- "Blowing bubbles is an art!"
- "Sometimes, happiness is just a bubble away."
- "Did you know fish use bubbles to communicate?"
- "Feeling bubbly today! How's your day going?"
- "In a world full of waves, be a bubble."

4. Feedback: Share the captions with friends or family for refinement or confirmation.

By mastering the art of captioning, you enhance the content and create a deeper connection with your audience.

CHAPTER 3: ENGAGING PLATFORMS

"It's not just about being seen; it's about being remembered."

Choosing the right platform for your pet's content is crucial.

Each platform has its own audience, style, and algorithms. This chapter will guide you through the most popular social media platforms, their strengths, and how to tailor your content to each.

11. Instagram: The Pet Paradise

"Where every whisker, feather, and fin finds its spotlight."

Harnessing Instagram's Visual Power

Instagram's emphasis on visuals, combined with its vast user base, makes it a prime platform for pet influencers. From curated feeds to spontaneous stories, Instagram offers myriad ways to share your pet's charm with the world.

Examples and Tips for Instagram:

1. Hashtag Power: Hashtags can significantly boost the visibility of your posts. For a photo of a dog playing in the park, consider using hashtags like #ParkPlaytime, #DogsofInstagram, or #HappyPup. Remember to mix popular hashtags with more niche ones to maximize reach.

2. Engagement is Key: If someone comments, "Such a cute pose!", respond with something like, "Thank you! It's one of his favorite spots to relax." Engaging with your audience builds a sense of community and encourages more interactions.

3. Stories Showcase: Use Instagram Stories to share moments that might not fit your main feed's aesthetic. If your pet is trying a new toy, a quick story with a caption like, "New toy alert!" can be both engaging and spontaneous.

4. Highlights for Evergreen Content: Use the Highlights feature to categorize and showcase evergreen content. For instance, if you often share tips on pet care, create a highlight titled "Pet Tips" where followers can easily access this valuable information.

5. Collaborations and Shoutouts: Engage with other pet accounts or brands. A shoutout exchange or a collaborative post can introduce your pet to a broader audience. For example, if you use a specific brand of pet food, a post showcasing mealtime with a caption like, "Dinner time with [Brand Name]! #Yum" can be a subtle way to collaborate.

Action Step:

1. Photo Selection: Choose a high-quality photo or video that captures your pet's personality.

2. Crafting the Caption: Based on the content, create an engaging caption. For a cat lounging in sunlight, consider something like, "Soaking up the sun and the attention. ☀️□"

3. Hashtag Research: Use tools like Display Purposes or check similar pet accounts to find relevant hashtags. Incorporate a mix of general (#CatsOfInstagram) and specific (#SunlitWhiskers) hashtags.

4. Post and Engage: After posting, spend some time engaging with followers. Respond to comments, visit profiles of those who engage with your content, and reciprocate the love.

Instagram, with its visual-centric approach and interactive features, provides a canvas for pet influencers to paint their stories, one post at a time. By understanding its nuances and leveraging its tools, your pet's account can flourish and resonate with a global audience.

12. TikTok: Short Clips, Big Impact

"Where every tail wag, wing flap, or playful pounce can become the next viral sensation."

Tapping into TikTok's Viral Nature

TikTok's bite-sized video format, combined with its unique algorithm, offers a level playing field for content creators. A single engaging video can catapult a pet to internet stardom, making it a platform ripe with potential for pet influencers.

Examples and Tips for TikTok:

1. Duration Matters: While TikTok allows videos up to 3 minutes, shorter clips often perform better due to the platform's fast-scrolling nature. A 15-second clip of a pet reacting hilariously to a new toy can be more engaging than a longer, drawn-out video.

2. Trend Participation: TikTok thrives on trends. If there's a trending challenge where people dance to a specific song, consider adapting it for your pet. For instance, if the trend involves sudden movements, a clip of your pet's amusing reactions to your dance can be both relevant and entertaining.

3. Music Makes a Difference: TikTok is as much about music as it is about visuals. A playful video paired with a dramatic soundtrack can add a humorous twist. Conversely, a serene clip of a pet sleeping paired with an upbeat track can create a fun juxtaposition.

4. Engage, Engage, Engage: TikTok's algorithm values engagement. If someone comments, "That jump was epic!", respond with something playful like, "He's been practicing his leap skills!" Engaging with comments not only builds community but can also boost your video's visibility.

5. Useful Captions: While TikTok is video-centric, captions can provide context or add humor. For a video of a pet chasing its tail, a caption like, "Going in circles trying to figure out Monday like..." can be relatable and funny.

Action Step:

1. Scout Trends: Spend some time on TikTok's "For You Page" to identify current trends, challenges, or popular songs.

2. Plan Your Video: Based on your observations, decide on a video concept. It could be your pet's version of a popular challenge or a unique reaction video.

3. Film Multiple Takes: Pets are unpredictable. It might take a few tries to get the perfect shot. Remember to keep it fun and stress-free for your pet.

4. Editing and Music: Use TikTok's in-app editing tools to trim the video, add effects, or incorporate music. Ensure the music complements the video's mood.

5. Post and Interact: Once you've uploaded the video, monitor the comments and engage with viewers. Sharing your video on other platforms can also increase its reach.

TikTok offers a dynamic and interactive platform where even the simplest moments can become internet gold. By understanding its trends and leveraging its features, pet influencers can create content that resonates, entertains, and goes viral.

13. YouTube: For the Pet Vlogger

"Where every purr, bark, and chirp becomes part of a visual narrative."

Diving Deep with YouTube

YouTube allows for in-depth storytelling, making it an ideal platform for those who wish to share more extensive content about their pets. From detailed tutorials to heartwarming stories, YouTube provides the canvas for pet influencers to paint a vivid picture.

Examples and Tips for YouTube:

1. Quality Over Quantity: Given the longer format, viewers expect better video and audio quality on YouTube. For instance, if you're filming a tutorial on training techniques, clear visuals of the steps and crisp audio explaining the process are essential.

2. Thumbnail Magic: Thumbnails act as the front cover of your video. An engaging thumbnail of your pet doing something intriguing, paired with bold text like "Epic Tricks!" or "Day in My Life," can significantly increase click-through rates.

3. Engage with Your Audience: YouTube isn't just about posting videos; it's a community. Responding to comments like, "Your pet is so talented!" with appreciative remarks such as, "Thank you! We've been practicing a lot!" can foster a loyal subscriber base.

4. Consistent Branding: Use intros, outros, and consistent graphics to create a recognizable brand for your channel. If every video starts with a cheerful jingle and a clip of your pet's playful antics, viewers will come to associate that with your brand.

5. Diverse Content: While having a niche is essential, diversifying within that niche keeps subscribers engaged. If your primary content is about pet care, occasionally posting a "fun day out" vlog or a "Q&A session" can offer fresh content to viewers.

Action Step:

1. Content Brainstorm: Decide on the theme of your 5-minute video. Is it a tutorial on a specific trick? A compilation of your pet's funniest moments? Or perhaps a narrative of a special day you spent together?

2. Storyboarding: Roughly plan the scenes or segments. For a tutorial, list down the steps. For a day-in-the-life video, jot down the activities you want to cover.

3. Filming: Ensure good lighting and clear audio. Film multiple takes if necessary to get the best shots. Remember to keep the process enjoyable for your pet.

4. Editing: Use software like Adobe Premiere Pro, Final Cut Pro, or even free tools like Shotcut to edit the video. Add transitions, text overlays, and background music to enhance the content.

5. Uploading and Engaging: Once uploaded, craft an engaging title and description. Use relevant tags to increase discoverability. Share the video on other platforms and engage with comments on YouTube to boost its reach.

YouTube offers a platform for in-depth engagement and storytelling. By focusing on quality content, consistent branding, and active community engagement, pet influencers can create a dedicated space where viewers return for their regular dose of furry, feathery, or scaly content.

14. Twitter: Quick Updates and Witty Remarks

"140 characters, endless possibilities for pet tales."

Tweeting the Pet Life

Twitter's fast-paced, text-centric nature might seem more suited for news and commentary, but it's also a platform where wit, humor, and real-time engagement shine. For pet influencers, it's a space to share bite-sized anecdotes, engage with fans, and even showcase short clips or photos.

Examples and Tips for Twitter:

1. Brevity is Key: Given Twitter's character limit, it's essential to be concise. A tweet like, "Tried teaching him a new trick. He taught me patience instead. #PetLife" encapsulates a story in just a few words.

2. Hashtag Usage: Hashtags can increase the discoverability of tweets. If you're tweeting about a lazy day with your pet, adding hashtags like #LazySunday or #PetChill can help reach a broader audience.

3. Engage with Trends: Twitter is all about what's happening now. If there's a trending topic that you can relate to your pet, jump in! For instance, during a sports event, a tweet like, "He's more interested in the ball than the game! #GameNight" can be both timely and engaging.

4. Photos and Clips: While Twitter is text-centric, visuals can enhance engagement. A cute photo or a short clip with a witty caption can stand out in the feed.

5. Interactions Matter: Engaging with followers or other accounts can boost your presence. If someone comments, "Your pet is adorable!", a simple "Thank you! He's quite the charmer." can foster positive interactions.

Action Step: Draft three tweets showcasing different aspects of your pet's personality or daily life.

1. Morning Antics: "Woke up to find him wearing my socks... again. Who needs an alarm when you have a fashion-forward pet? #MorningSurprises"

2. Mealtime Drama: "Decided to try a new pet food flavor. The verdict? A stare that says, 'Bring back the old one, human.' #DinnerTimeDebates"

3. Playful Evenings: "Bought a new toy. It's been 5 minutes, and it's already MIA. Detective mode: ON! #HideAndSeekChampion"

Twitter offers a unique space for pet influencers to share quick updates, engage in real-time, and showcase their pet's personality in bite-sized anecdotes. By understanding the platform's dynamics and leveraging its features, pet influencers can create a vibrant and engaging Twitter presence.

15. Facebook: Building a Community

"Where every 'like' and 'share' weaves a tale of tails and whiskers."

Fostering Connections on Facebook

Facebook's diverse tools and features make it an ideal platform for pet influencers looking to build a more intimate and engaged community. From sharing detailed stories to hosting live sessions, Facebook offers myriad ways to connect with fans and foster a sense of belonging.

Examples and Tips for Facebook:

1. Diverse Content: Unlike platforms that emphasize a specific content type, Facebook thrives on variety. A photo album titled "Beach Day Adventures," a video of a new trick, or a heartfelt text post about a memorable moment can all find a home on Facebook.

2. Engagement Opportunities: Use Facebook's interactive features to engage with your audience. For instance, if you're considering buying a new toy or accessory, run a poll asking for recommendations. Or post a photo with a caption like, "Caption this!" to invite creative responses.

3. Live Sessions: Facebook Live offers a real-time connection with your audience. Consider hosting a live Q&A session, a behind-the-scenes look at your day, or even a live training session. The spontaneous interactions can strengthen the bond with your community.

4. Groups for Deeper Engagement: Creating a group for your pet's fans can be a game-changer. It's a space where fans can share their own pet stories, photos, and bond over shared experiences. Regularly engaging in the group, sharing exclusive content, or even hosting group-specific events can make members feel valued.

5. Consistent Interactions: On Facebook, consistency is crucial. Regular posts, timely responses to comments, and active participation in discussions can keep the community vibrant and engaged.

Action Step:

1. Engagement Post: Craft a post that invites interaction. For example: "Happy Friday, everyone! We're curious: What's one quirky habit your pet has? Share your stories in the comments! ❤☐"

2. Engage Actively: As responses start pouring in, engage with them. If someone shares, "My cat loves to knock over empty boxes," respond with something like, "Haha, classic cat move! Thanks for sharing."

3. Encourage Sharing: Occasionally, prompt your followers to share photos or videos in response to your posts. For instance, "It's #SunnySunday! How are you and your pets enjoying the day? Share your sunny snaps below! ☀☐"

Facebook, with its community-centric approach, offers pet influencers a platform to not just share content but to build meaningful relationships with their audience. By leveraging its features and maintaining active engagement, influencers can create a thriving, supportive, and interactive community.

Choosing the right platform is about understanding where your audience is and tailoring your content to that platform's strengths. As you grow, you might expand to other platforms, but it's essential to start where you can maintain consistency and quality. Remember, it's not about being everywhere; it's about being impactful where you are.

CHAPTER 4: MONETIZING YOUR PET'S FAME

"Turn your pet's paw prints into profit, ethically and responsibly."

As your pet gains popularity, there will be opportunities to monetize their online presence. This chapter will guide you through understanding sponsored content, partnering with brands, and diversifying your income streams while ensuring your pet's well-being.

16. Understanding Sponsored Content

"Where brand partnerships meet genuine pet love."

Navigating the World of Sponsored Content

As your pet gains popularity, brands might see potential in collaborating with you. While this can be exciting and financially rewarding, it's crucial to approach sponsored content with caution and integrity. Your audience trusts you, and maintaining that trust should be paramount.

Examples and Tips for Sponsored Content:

1. Authenticity is Key: If you're approached by a brand selling a type of pet food that you wouldn't feed your pet, it's best to decline the offer. For instance, if you've always promoted organic pet food and a brand selling non-organic products approaches you, promoting their product might come off as disingenuous.

2. Transparency with Your Audience: Platforms often have guidelines about disclosing sponsored content. Beyond that, being open with your audience about partnerships fosters trust. A simple "Excited to partner with [Brand Name] for this post!" can suffice.

3. Prioritize Your Pet's Well-being: If a brand wants to send a product for your pet to try, ensure it's safe and suitable for them. For instance, if a brand offers a toy for a large dog breed and you have a small dog, it might not be appropriate.

4. Understand the Terms: Before agreeing to any collaboration, understand what the brand expects. How many posts? What kind of content? Do they want to review the content before it goes live? Knowing these details upfront can prevent misunderstandings later.

5. Stay True to Your Voice: Even when creating sponsored content, it should feel like any other post on your platform. If your posts are usually light-hearted and funny, a sudden serious tone might feel out of place to your followers.

Action Step:

1. Dream Brand List: Jot down brands or products that align with your pet's lifestyle and your values. For instance:

   - Organic Pet Food Brands: If you've always emphasized natural nutrition.

   - Eco-friendly Toy Brands: If sustainability is a value you uphold.

- Pet Wellness Products: Such as supplements or grooming tools that you believe would benefit your pet.

- Pet Fashion Brands: If your pet has a flair for fashion and you often showcase outfits or accessories.

- Pet Travel Accessories: If you often share adventures or trips with your pet.

2. Research and Outreach: Once you have a list, research these brands. Do they collaborate with influencers? What's their reputation? If they align with your values, consider reaching out proactively with a proposal.

Sponsored content offers a way to monetize your pet's online presence, but it's essential to approach it with integrity and authenticity. By aligning with brands that share your values and being transparent with your audience, you can create sponsored content that feels genuine and maintains trust.

17. Partnering with Pet Brands

"Where your pet's charm meets brand charisma."

Building Beneficial Brand Partnerships

As the world of pet influencers grows, brands recognize the value of partnering with genuine voices in the community. These collaborations can provide value to the brand, the influencer, and the audience. However, navigating these partnerships requires research, clarity, and authenticity.

Examples and Tips for Partnering with Pet Brands:

1. Due Diligence: Before agreeing to any partnership, research the brand. Look into customer reviews, product recalls, or any controversies. For instance, if you're considering a partnership with a pet food brand, understanding its ingredients, sourcing practices, and customer feedback is crucial.

2. Clear Contracts: A well-defined contract protects both parties. It should outline the scope of work, compensation (monetary, products, or both), content approval processes, and any other expectations. For example, if a brand expects three Instagram posts and two Stories, this should be clearly stated and agreed upon.

3. Authentic Promotions: Your audience follows you for genuine content. When promoting a brand, share real experiences. If a toy became your pet's favorite, showcase that. If a product didn't quite match your expectations, it's okay to provide constructive feedback.

4. Engage with the Brand: Beyond the contractual obligations, engage with the brand on social media. Share their posts, participate in their campaigns, and foster a relationship beyond the partnership.

5. Feedback Loop: After a promotional campaign, provide feedback to the brand. Share metrics, audience reactions, and any insights that might help in future collaborations.

Action Step:

1. Crafting a Proposal: When reaching out to a brand, ensure your proposal is professional and compelling. Here's a template to consider:

- Introduction: "Hello [Brand Name], I'm [Your Name], and my pet [Pet's Name] has a growing following on [Platform]. We love your products and believe there's potential for a great collaboration."

- Highlight Metrics: "With over [X number] of engaged followers and an average engagement rate of [X%], our audience trusts our recommendations and loves seeing new products in action."

- Proposal Idea: "We'd love to showcase [specific product] in a series of posts, highlighting its benefits and our genuine experiences."

- Closing: "We believe this partnership could be beneficial for both of us. Looking forward to discussing this further and exploring potential collaboration avenues."

2. Follow-Up: If you don't hear back within a week or two, consider sending a polite follow-up email. Brands often receive numerous proposals, and a gentle reminder can bring yours to their attention.

Partnering with pet brands can be a rewarding experience, both in terms of content diversity and potential revenue. By approaching these partnerships with research, clarity, and authenticity, pet influencers can ensure that collaborations are beneficial for all parties involved.

18. Selling Pet-Themed Merchandise

"From screens to tangible keepsakes, where your pet's charm becomes a cherished item."

Turning Popularity into Products

As your pet's online presence grows, there's potential to monetize beyond brand partnerships. Merchandise offers a tangible way for fans to showcase their love for your pet and can become a significant revenue stream if done right.

Examples and Tips for Pet-Themed Merchandise:

1. Quality Over Quantity: It's essential to ensure that any merchandise you produce is of high quality. Whether it's a soft, durable t-shirt or a mug with a print that doesn't fade, quality products will enhance your brand's reputation. For instance, if you're selling a calendar, using high-resolution images and quality paper can make a difference.

2. Unique Designs: Collaborate with artists or graphic designers to create designs that stand out. If your pet has a signature pose or a memorable expression, that could be turned into a quirky illustration. For example, a playful sketch of your pet with a caption like "Mondays, am I right?" can resonate with many.

*3. Organic Promotion: I*nstead of hard-selling, integrate merchandise promotions seamlessly into your content. Wearing the t-shirt in a post or sipping from the branded mug in a video can be subtle yet effective ways to showcase the products.

4. Limited Editions: Consider launching limited edition merchandise for special occasions or milestones. For instance, a "Birthday Special" t-shirt or a "Holiday Edition" mug can create urgency and exclusivity.

5. Engage with Fans: Encourage fans who purchase your merchandise to share photos of them using or wearing the products. This not only acts as user-generated content but also builds a sense of community.

Action Step:

1. Merchandise Ideas:

   - Pet Planner: A yearly planner featuring cute photos of your pet for each month, along with stickers or quotes.

   - Signature Pose T-shirt: A t-shirt showcasing a popular or signature pose of your pet with a catchy caption.

   - Mug Series: A series of mugs, each with a different expression of your pet, like "Morning Mood," "Midday Slump," and "Evening Vibes."

2. Gauge Interest: Post a teaser or a mock-up of one of the merchandise ideas on your platform with a caption like, "Thinking of launching some fun merch! Which one would you love to have?" Conduct a poll or ask for feedback in the comments to understand what resonates most with your audience.

Selling pet-themed merchandise allows fans to have a piece of their favorite online pet in their daily lives. By ensuring quality, creating unique designs, and promoting products organically, pet influencers can turn their pet's charm into cherished keepsakes for their audience.

19. Affiliate Marketing for Pet Products

"Where genuine recommendations meet rewarding commissions."

Monetizing Through Recommendations

Affiliate marketing is a popular way for influencers to monetize their platforms. For pet influencers, this can be especially lucrative given the vast array of pet products available. However, it's essential to approach affiliate marketing with authenticity to maintain trust with your audience.

Examples and Tips for Affiliate Marketing:

1. Authentic Recommendations: Only promote products you've tried and believe in. For instance, if you've been using a particular brand of pet food that your pet loves and thrives on, it makes sense to become an affiliate for that brand.

2. Natural Integration: Instead of creating content around affiliate products, integrate them naturally into your existing content. For example, in a post about your pet's bedtime routine, you can mention and link to their favorite chew toy that helps them relax.

3. Transparency is Key: Many platforms and regions have regulations about disclosing affiliate relationships. Even if they didn't, it's good practice to be transparent. A simple note like, "The link below is an affiliate link, which means I might earn a small commission if you make a purchase, at no extra cost to you," can maintain trust.

4. Track Performance: Most affiliate programs offer analytics. Monitor which products your audience prefers and the type of content that drives more sales. This can help you refine your strategy over time.

5. Stay Updated: Affiliate programs often have promotions, discounts, or special offers. Staying updated allows you to provide timely recommendations to your audience, increasing the chances of conversions.

Action Step:

1. Research and Join: Look into popular pet product affiliate programs. Websites like Amazon, Chewy, or Petco often have affiliate programs with a wide range of products. Join a program that aligns with your content and audience preferences.

2. Test Products: Before promoting, try out products to ensure they meet your standards. Document the experience, as real-life testimonials can be more convincing than generic promotions.

3. Promotion Ideas:

   - Product Reviews: A detailed review, discussing the pros and cons, can provide value to your audience and drive sales.

   - Tutorials or How-to's: If it's a product that requires demonstration, like a pet grooming tool, a tutorial can be both educational and promotional.

   - Favorites List: A monthly or seasonal list of your pet's favorite products can be a recurring segment that integrates affiliate links.

Affiliate marketing offers a way for pet influencers to monetize their genuine product recommendations. By choosing products that align with their brand, integrating links naturally, and being transparent about affiliate relationships, influencers can earn commissions while providing value to their audience.

20. Setting up a Patreon or Fan Subscription Model

"Where fans become patrons, and exclusive tales unfold."

Deepening the Connection with Dedicated Fans

Platforms like Patreon provide a unique opportunity for creators to offer exclusive content and experiences to their most dedicated fans. For pet influencers, this can mean sharing special moments, insights, or even tangible rewards with those who are willing to support their journey.

Examples and Tips for Patreon:

1. Tiered Support: Offer different levels of support, each with its own set of perks. For instance:

- Bronze Tier ($3/month): Access to exclusive photos.

- Silver Tier ($5/month): Above perks + behind-the-scenes videos.

- Gold Tier ($10/month): All of the above + a monthly live Q&A session.

2. Exclusive Content: This is the heart of Patreon. Whether it's a special video series, unseen photos, or personal updates, ensure that the content you offer is unique and not available on your regular platforms.

3. Engage with Patrons: Your patrons are your most dedicated fans. Engage with them, ask for feedback, and make them feel valued. For instance, you could have a monthly "Ask Me Anything" session or polls to decide on future content.

4. Tangible Rewards: Depending on your tier structure, consider sending physical rewards. This could be a handwritten thank-you note, stickers, or even a calendar featuring your pet.

5. Organic Promotion: Instead of hard-selling your Patreon, integrate its promotion into your content. Share snippets of what patrons receive, or occasionally mention the platform when relevant. For example, after sharing a fun video, you could add, "Want to see the bloopers from today's antics? They're up on our Patreon!"

Action Step:

1. Setting Up Your Patreon:

- Profile: Use a clear profile picture of your pet and a banner that represents your content.

- Description: Write a heartfelt description explaining why you've set up the Patreon, what supporters can expect, and how their support helps.

- Tiers: Set up at least three tiers with clear descriptions of the perks. Ensure that the rewards are manageable for you to deliver consistently.

- Launch Content: Before promoting your Patreon, have some exclusive content ready. This ensures that early supporters immediately see value.

2. Promotion Ideas:

- Teaser Posts: Share snippets or previews of Patreon-exclusive content on your regular platforms.

- Testimonials: If patrons are loving the exclusive content, ask them for testimonials or feedback and share these (with permission).

- Milestones: Celebrate milestones (e.g., reaching 50 patrons) with special posts or shoutouts.

Setting up a Patreon or fan subscription model allows creators to deepen their connection with their most dedicated fans. By offering exclusive content, engaging regularly, and providing tangible rewards, pet influencers can build a supportive community that directly contributes to their journey.

CHAPTER 5: BEYOND THE SCREEN

"From pixels to the real world: Expanding your pet's influence."

While the digital realm offers vast opportunities, there's a world beyond the screen where your pet can make an impact. This chapter delves into real-world opportunities, from attending conventions to collaborating with local businesses.

21. Attending Pet Conventions and Meet-Ups

"From the digital realm to real-world rendezvous."

Expanding Your Network in the Physical World

While the digital space offers vast opportunities for growth and engagement, there's something special about face-to-face interactions. Pet conventions and meet-ups provide a unique setting to connect with like-minded individuals, brands, and dedicated fans.

Examples and Tips for Attending Pet Conventions:

1. Media Kit Preparation: Your media kit is like a resume. It should highlight your pet's online metrics, notable collaborations, audience demographics, and contact information. For instance, if your pet has 50,000 Instagram followers with a 10% engagement rate, that's a key metric to highlight.

2. Engaging with Brands: Conventions often have booths set up by various pet brands. Engage with them, introduce yourself, and explore potential collaboration opportunities. For example, if you've been using a specific brand's product and genuinely love it, share your experience with them; it could lead to a partnership.

3. Fan Meet-and-Greets: If you have a sizable local following, consider organizing a meet-and-greet. It's a chance for fans to meet your pet in person and for you to express gratitude for their support. Ensure you choose a pet-friendly location and consider factors like safety and crowd management.

4. Stay Updated: Conventions often have panels, workshops, or talks. Attend sessions that resonate with you. Whether it's about pet wellness, content creation, or brand collaborations, there's always something new to learn.

5. Document the Experience: Share your convention journey with your online audience. From behind-the-scenes preparations to highlights of the day, it's content that your followers would love to see.

6. Networking: Beyond brands and fans, conventions are a great place to connect with fellow pet influencers. Share experiences, learn from each other, and even consider potential collaborations.

Action Step:

1. Research and Planning: Look for upcoming pet conventions, expos, or events in your region. Websites, pet forums, or local pet communities can be good starting points.

2. Preparation: Once you've decided on an event:

- Logistics: Book tickets, arrange transportation, and ensure the event is pet-friendly if you plan to bring your pet.

- Promotion: Announce on your platforms that you'll be attending. If you're planning a meet-and-greet, provide details like time and location.

- Media Kit: Update your media kit. Consider getting it printed in a professional format to hand out at the event.

Attending pet conventions and meet-ups can be a rewarding experience, both professionally and personally. It offers a chance to step out of the digital realm, forge real-world connections, and immerse oneself in the vibrant pet community.

22. Guest Appearances on TV Shows or Commercials

"From social media stardom to the silver screen."

Stepping into the Limelight with Your Pet

The transition from social media to traditional media like TV can be a significant leap. It offers a broader audience reach and can cement your pet's status as a bona fide star. However, navigating this space requires preparation and ensuring your pet's comfort at all times.

Examples and Tips for Media Appearances:

1. Comfort First: TV sets can be overwhelming with bright lights, multiple people, and loud noises. Ensure that the environment is pet-friendly. For instance, if your pet is sensitive to loud sounds, check if the studio can accommodate a quieter setting or if you can bring noise-cancelling earmuffs for your pet.

2. Rehearse: If your pet is performing a trick or showcasing a skill, practice in advance. Familiarity can help reduce stress during the actual appearance.

3. Prepare Talking Points: Whether you're being interviewed or your pet is the main focus, have a set of talking points ready. This could include your pet's backstory, their journey to fame, or any causes you're passionate about, like pet adoption.

4. Stay Authentic: While TV appearances can be more structured than social media, maintain the authenticity that made your pet popular in the first place. If your pet isn't in the mood to perform a trick, it's okay. Share a funny anecdote instead.

5. Promotion: Leverage your social media platforms to promote your TV appearance. Share behind-the-scenes snippets, announce the airing date, and engage with fans who tune in to watch.

6. Rights and Permissions: Ensure you understand and agree with how the footage will be used. If it's a commercial, are they allowed to use it only for a specific duration? Will it be broadcast internationally? Clarify these details in advance.

Action Step:

1. Crafting Your Pitch:

   - Introduction: Start with a brief introduction about yourself and your pet.

   - Highlight Achievements: Mention any significant milestones, like follower count, brand collaborations, or previous media appearances.

   - Unique Selling Point: What makes your pet stand out? Is it a specific trick, a heartwarming backstory, or their infectious personality?

   - Proposal: Clearly state what you're offering, whether it's a guest appearance, a segment idea, or participation in a commercial.

   - Contact Details: Ensure you provide a way for them to reach out to you.

2. Research and Outreach: Identify TV shows, segments, or commercials that align with your pet's brand. Local morning shows, talk shows, or even pet-specific programs can be a good start. Once you have a list, send out your pitch, and be patient. It might take time, but one positive response can kickstart your pet's TV career.

Making a TV appearance can be a game-changer in your pet's influencer journey. By ensuring their comfort, preparing adequately, and promoting the appearance, you can make the most of this opportunity and reach new heights of popularity.

23. Publishing a Pet Calendar or Photo Book

"Preserving Paw-some Memories in Print."

Immersing Fans in a Year of Pet Perfection

Calendars and photo books offer fans a tangible way to cherish their favorite pet influencer's moments throughout the year. It's an opportunity to showcase your pet's charm, create a keepsake for fans, and even earn revenue through sales.

Examples and Tips for Publishing:

1. Professional Photography: Collaborate with a professional pet photographer to capture your pet's best moments. Their expertise in lighting, composition, and pet handling can elevate the quality of the final product.

2. Theme and Layout: Decide on a theme for the calendar or photo book. It could revolve around seasons, holidays, or specific activities your pet enjoys. As for the layout, ensure it's aesthetically pleasing and user-friendly.

3. Printing Quality: Invest in high-quality printing. Choose thick, glossy paper for calendars and consider hardcover options for photo books. The tactile experience adds value to the product.

4. Preparation and Promotion: Plan well in advance for a smooth release. Set a timeline for photography, design, and printing. Promote the upcoming release on your social media platforms to generate excitement and anticipation.

5. Distribution: Decide on the distribution channels for your calendar or photo book. You can sell them through your website, partner with local pet stores, or collaborate with online marketplaces.

6. Limited Editions: Consider offering limited editions with additional perks, like a signed copy, a personalized message, or even a special packaging.

Action Step:

1. Selecting Photos: Gather your best pet photos from your archive. Choose 12 images that represent your pet's personality and showcase their unique charm.

2. Layout Mock-up: Create a mock-up of the calendar or photo book layout. Consider the arrangement of photos, spacing, and any additional text or captions.

3. Photographer Collaboration: If you haven't worked with a professional pet photographer before, research and reach out to find a photographer whose style aligns with your vision.

4. Promotion Plan: Outline your promotion strategy. Decide on release dates, teaser posts, behind-the-scenes content, and how you'll announce availability for pre-orders.

Publishing a pet calendar or photo book allows you to share your pet's captivating moments beyond the digital world. By collaborating with professionals, ensuring quality, and promoting well in advance, you can create a cherished keepsake for your fans while further establishing your pet's brand.

24. Launching Pet-Centric Events or Workshops

"Bringing the Pet Community Together, One Paw-some Event at a Time."

Creating Unforgettable Pet Experiences

Hosting pet-centric events or workshops not only deepens your pet's connection with their fans but also fosters a sense of community among pet lovers. From educational workshops to fun-themed parties, events provide an opportunity to showcase your pet's influence beyond the virtual space.

Examples and Tips for Hosting Pet-Centric Events:

1. Event Themes: Consider the interests and preferences of your pet's audience. Some event ideas could include a pet care workshop, a pet costume contest, a charity fundraiser, or a pet adoption drive.

2. Collaborations and Sponsorships: Partner with local businesses or pet-related organizations for sponsorships or co-hosting. They can provide resources, venue space, or even financial support, making the event more impactful.

3. Safety and Pet-Friendliness: Ensure that the event environment is safe and suitable for pets. This includes having designated pet rest areas, providing water and shade, and adhering to local pet regulations.

4. Promotion and Outreach: Utilize your social media platforms to extensively promote the event. Create eye-catching graphics, engaging posts, and share behind-the-scenes preparations. Leverage your pet's influence to generate excitement and encourage attendance.

5. Engaging Activities: Plan activities that involve pets and their owners. For example, at a pet care workshop, you could demonstrate grooming techniques or offer training tips. At a themed party, organize pet-friendly games or contests.

6. Event Souvenirs: Consider offering event souvenirs, such as branded pet toys, t-shirts, or bandanas. Not only do they act as mementos, but they also serve as additional marketing for your pet's brand.

Action Step:

1. Event Concept: Brainstorm an event idea that aligns with your pet's brand and the interests of your audience. For instance, if your pet is known for their fashion sense, a pet fashion show could be a hit.

2. Logistics and Collaborations: Outline the logistics, such as event date, location, and potential collaborators. Reach out to local businesses, pet-related organizations, or even fellow pet influencers who might be interested in participating.

3. Budget and Sponsorships: Create a budget for the event and identify potential sources of sponsorship or funding. This could include local pet stores, grooming salons, or pet food brands.

4. Promotion Plan: Plan a comprehensive promotion strategy, including teaser posts, behind-the-scenes content, and announcements. Encourage your followers to share the event details to increase reach.

5. Event Execution: Ensure all arrangements, such as permits, safety measures, and logistics, are in place for a smooth event experience.

Hosting pet-centric events or workshops can strengthen your pet's influence and create memorable experiences for their fans. By collaborating with local businesses, prioritizing safety and pet-friendliness, and promoting extensively, your pet can leave a paw-print on the hearts of attendees.

25. Collaborating with Local Pet Businesses

"Fostering Pawsitive Partnerships in Your Neighborhood."

Building Bridges in the Local Pet Community

Collaborating with local pet businesses can be a win-win for both parties involved. It allows your pet to support and promote businesses in their local community while gaining access to products, services, or opportunities that enhance their influence.

Examples and Tips for Local Collaborations:

1. Promotional Exchanges: Reach out to local pet stores, groomers, cafes, or pet-friendly venues and propose a collaboration. Offer to promote their business on your social media platforms in exchange for their products or services.

2. Joint Events or Promotions: Plan joint events or promotions to draw in more customers. For example, you could host a pet meet-and-greet at a local pet store, where customers can meet your pet while browsing products.

3. Social Media Takeovers: Partner with a local pet-related business for a social media takeover. Your pet can spend a day at the business, sharing behind-the-scenes content and engaging with their audience.

4. Cause-Related Collaborations: Align with pet businesses that support charitable causes related to animals. Organize a charity event or campaign together to raise funds or awareness for a shared cause.

5. Product Reviews: Collaborate with local pet stores to review their products. Honest reviews provide value to your audience and can attract potential customers to the store.

6. Sponsorship Opportunities: If your pet is hosting an event or workshop, consider reaching out to local businesses for sponsorship. They can provide supplies, treats, or goodie bags for attendees.

Action Step:

1. Identify Local Pet Businesses: List down local pet-related businesses in your area. This could include pet stores, grooming salons, pet cafes, or pet-friendly venues.

2. Research and Familiarize: Research each business to understand their offerings, target audience, and brand values. Familiarize yourself with their social media presence and recent events or promotions.

3. Draft a Collaboration Proposal: Tailor a collaboration proposal for one of the businesses. Highlight the benefits of the collaboration, such as increased exposure and potential customer engagement.

4. Reach Out: Contact the business through email or social media with your collaboration proposal. Be professional and courteous in your approach.

5. Follow Up: If you don't receive an immediate response, don't be discouraged. Follow up politely after a week or two to reiterate your interest in collaborating.

Collaborating with local pet businesses can enrich your pet's influence within the community and strengthen ties with fellow pet lovers. By offering promotional exchanges, organizing joint events, and ensuring the collaboration aligns with your pet's brand, you create a supportive network of pet-centric partners.

CHAPTER 6: CHALLENGES AND SOLUTIONS

"Every challenge is an opportunity in disguise."

T he journey of turning your pet into an influencer isn't without its hurdles. This chapter will address potential challenges you might face and provide solutions to navigate them gracefully.

26. Dealing with Negative Comments or Trolls

"Navigating the Storm: Shielding Your Pet's Influence."

Maintaining Positivity Amidst Online Challenges

While being a pet influencer comes with numerous joys, it also exposes your pet to potential negativity from internet trolls or negative comments. It's essential to protect your pet's well-being and preserve the positive atmosphere of their online community.

Examples and Tips for Handling Negativity:

1. Avoid Engaging with Trolls: Trolls seek attention and thrive on negative reactions. It's best not to respond to their comments as engaging may escalate the situation further. Instead, focus on uplifting and engaging with your supportive followers.

2. Focus on Positivity: For every negative comment, there are countless positive and supportive ones. Concentrate on the love and appreciation you receive from your loyal fanbase.

3. Delete or Hide Inappropriate Comments: Most social media platforms allow you to delete or hide comments. Use this feature for any comments that are offensive, abusive, or inappropriate.

4. Block and Report: If you encounter persistent or harmful trolls, use the platform's blocking and reporting features. This helps protect not only your pet but also your followers from negativity.

5. Support from Followers: Encourage your followers to report and stand up against trolls and negativity. A united community can help drown out negative voices.

6. Utilize Filters: Set up filters to automatically hide or review comments that contain potentially harmful or negative words. This can help shield your pet and followers from hurtful content.

Action Step:

1. Review Platform Settings: Familiarize yourself with the privacy and comment settings on each platform your pet is active on. Enable comment moderation if available.

2. Filter Words and Phrases: Identify potentially harmful or negative words and phrases that you'd like to filter out. Use the platform's settings to set up keyword filters.

3. Monitor and Adjust: Regularly review the comments on your posts to ensure the filters are working as intended. Adjust the filters as needed to refine their effectiveness.

Handling negative comments and trolls is an inevitable part of being an online influencer. By focusing on positivity, using platform tools to control comments, and creating a supportive community, you can ensure that your pet's online presence remains a space of joy and inspiration.

27. Ensuring Your Pet's Well-Being and Avoiding Overexposure

"Guardians of Joy: Nurturing Your Pet's Health and Happiness."

Balancing Fame and Well-Being

As your pet gains popularity as an influencer, it's crucial to strike a balance between their online presence and overall well-being. Prioritizing your pet's health, happiness, and comfort ensures they continue to thrive as the heart and soul of your pet-centric content.

Examples and Tips for Ensuring Well-Being:

1. Monitor Stress Signals: Pets communicate through body language and behavior. Pay attention to signs of stress, such as excessive panting, hiding, loss of appetite, or avoidance of certain activities. Adjust their exposure or schedule if you notice any signs of discomfort.

2. Limit Exposure: While sharing your pet's moments is part of being an influencer, it's vital to strike a balance. Avoid overexposing your pet with too frequent shoots, events, or appearances. Let them have ample downtime to recharge and enjoy regular playtime.

3. Quality Over Quantity: Focus on creating meaningful and engaging content rather than constantly churning out posts. Your pet's genuine moments and interactions with you and their environment will resonate more with your audience.

4. Safe and Pet-Friendly Environments: Whether it's events, meet-ups, or collaborations, ensure that any new environment your pet is exposed to is safe, pet-friendly, and comfortable for them.

5. Downtime and Bonding: Schedule regular downtime for your pet to relax and bond with you without the pressure of performing or posing for content.

6. Health Check-ups: Regular veterinary check-ups are essential to ensure your pet is in good health. Consult with your vet about their activities and any changes you notice in their behavior.

Action Step:

1. Assessment: Reflect on your pet's recent activities and engagements. Evaluate their behavior and any potential signs of stress or fatigue.

2. Scheduling and Prioritizing: Create a balanced schedule that includes ample downtime and bonding activities. Limit their participation in events or shoots to avoid overwhelming them.

3. Communication with Veterinarian: Schedule a vet check-up to discuss your pet's activities, any concerns you may have, and get professional advice on maintaining their well-being.

Guarding your pet's well-being is a responsibility that comes with their online influence. By monitoring their behavior, limiting exposure, and prioritizing their health and happiness, you ensure they continue to shine as the joyful and vibrant pet influencer they are.

28. Handling Copycats and Content Theft

"Protecting the Paw Prints of Originality."

Safeguarding Your Pet's Unique Voice

As your pet's influence grows, it's not uncommon for others to imitate or steal their content. Protecting your pet's originality and ensuring proper credit for their creative endeavors is crucial to maintaining their authenticity and credibility as a pet influencer.

Examples and Tips for Handling Copycats:

1. Watermark Your Content: Add a subtle watermark to your photos or videos that includes your pet's name or your social media handle. This helps identify your content and discourage others from claiming it as their own.

2. Reverse Image Search Tools: Utilize reverse image search tools, such as Google Images, to monitor for any unauthorized usage of your content. If you find instances of theft, take appropriate action.

3. Copyright and Licensing: Consider copyrighting your original content or exploring licensing options for its usage. This can offer legal protection and give you recourse if content theft occurs.

4. Polite Request for Credit or Removal: If you discover someone using your pet's content without permission, reach out to them politely and request either proper credit or the removal of the content.

5. Educate Your Audience: Encourage your loyal followers to report instances of content theft and educate them about the importance of supporting original creators.

6. Protect Your Social Media Accounts: Enable content protection features on your social media accounts to prevent unauthorized downloading or saving of your content.

Action Step:

1. Designing a Watermark: Create a subtle and visually appealing watermark that can be applied to your pet's photos or videos. Experiment with different placements and opacities to find what works best.

2. Implementing the Watermark: Apply the watermark to a selection of your pet's recent photos or videos. Ensure it doesn't distract from the main content while still being visible.

3. Monitoring Unauthorized Usage: Use reverse image search tools to search for instances of your content being used without permission. Take note of any instances you find.

4. Developing a Response Plan: Plan how you'll respond if you encounter content theft or copycats. Consider how you'll approach the individuals involved and what actions you'll take to protect your pet's content.

Protecting your pet's content from copycats and content theft is essential to maintain their unique voice and credibility in the online space. By watermarking your content, monitoring for unauthorized usage, and taking action against theft when necessary, you safeguard your pet's influence and preserve their originality.

29. Navigating the Changing Landscape of Social Media Algorithms

"Adapting and Thriving Amid Algorithmic Waves."

Staying Afloat in the Ever-Shifting Social Media Seas

Social media platforms are notorious for their ever-changing algorithms, which can significantly impact how content is displayed and reach your audience. Navigating these shifts requires vigilance, adaptability, and a focus on fostering genuine connections with your pet's audience.

Examples and Tips for Navigating Algorithm Changes:

1. Stay Informed: Regularly check for updates and announcements from social media platforms about algorithm changes. Platforms often provide insights or guidelines to help content creators adapt.

2. Engage with Your Audience: Social media algorithms tend to favor content that generates genuine engagement. Respond to comments, encourage discussions, and make your audience feel valued.

3. Consistent Posting: Regular and consistent posting can signal to algorithms that your content is active and relevant. Create a posting schedule that aligns with your audience's peak activity times.

4. Quality Over Quantity: Prioritize creating high-quality content that resonates with your pet's audience. Well-received content is more likely to gain visibility, even amidst algorithm changes.

5. Diversify Across Platforms: Relying heavily on a single platform can be risky. Diversify your pet's online presence across multiple platforms to reduce the impact of algorithm fluctuations.

6. Explore New Features: Social media platforms often introduce new features that they want to promote. Experiment with these features as they can provide a boost in visibility.

Action Step:

1. Platform-Specific Research: Research each social media platform where your pet is active and find official resources or forums where updates and algorithm changes are discussed.

2. Join Influencer Groups or Forums: Seek out online groups or forums where influencers discuss algorithm changes and strategies. Engage with other content creators to share insights and learn from their experiences.

3. Content Planning and Scheduling: Create a content plan that factors in algorithm changes and adapts to new trends or features. Schedule posts strategically to maximize visibility.

4. Audience Insights: Analyze your audience insights to understand when they are most active and engaged. Use this information to plan your posting schedule.

Adapting to the shifting algorithms of social media platforms is a constant challenge for pet influencers. By staying informed, engaging consistently with your audience, and diversifying your presence, you can navigate these changes and continue to build a strong and loyal following for your pet.

30. Balancing Fame with Privacy

"Guarding the Gates of Personal Boundaries."

Safeguarding Your Pet and Personal Space

As your pet's influence expands, it's essential to strike a balance between sharing their adorable moments with the world and protecting your personal life and privacy. Implementing thoughtful strategies to maintain a healthy boundary can help ensure your pet's fame doesn't encroach on your personal space.

Examples and Tips for Balancing Fame and Privacy:

1. Separate Personal and Pet Profiles: Keep personal details, such as your full name, address, and private life, off your pet's public profiles. Create a separate social media account for personal use.

2. Avoid Real-time Location Sharing: Be cautious about sharing your current location in real-time. Wait until you've left a location before posting about it to avoid potential safety concerns.

3. Set Boundaries with Followers: Be clear about what you're willing to share with your pet's audience. Decide in advance what aspects of your life will remain private and politely decline any inquiries that cross those boundaries.

4. Protect Your Pet's Safety: Refrain from sharing information that could potentially compromise your pet's safety, such as specific walking routes or routines.

5. Use General Terms: If you want to share personal stories or experiences, use general terms or share in a way that doesn't reveal too many specifics.

6. Monitor Tags and Mentions: Keep an eye on tags and mentions on social media to ensure that your pet is not linked to any private or personal content without your consent.

Action Step:

1. Profile Review: Conduct a thorough review of your pet's social media profiles. Remove any personal details or sensitive information that may inadvertently have been shared.

2. Discuss Boundaries: Have a conversation with your family or those close to you about the level of privacy you wish to maintain and agree on how to handle situations where your boundaries may be tested.

3. Social Media Cleanup: Regularly audit your pet's social media content to ensure that it aligns with your privacy preferences. Remove any posts or information that you no longer wish to share.

4. Stay Attentive: Continuously monitor your pet's social media presence to ensure that privacy boundaries are respected by followers, fans, and potential partners.

Maintaining a balance between your pet's fame and your privacy is essential for both your well-being and your pet's safety. By setting boundaries, being cautious about what you share, and regularly reviewing your pet's online presence, you can protect your personal life while continuing to delight your pet's audience with their adorable moments.

CHAPTER 7: THE FUTURE OF PET INFLUENCING

"Adapting, evolving, and paw-spering in the ever-changing digital landscape."

T he world of pet influencing, like all digital landscapes, is continually evolving. This chapter will guide you through keeping up with trends, transitioning from online fame to other ventures, and ensuring the lasting impact of your pet's online presence.

31. Embracing Change: Riding the Waves of Digital Evolution

"Surfing the Digital Tides: Embracing Trends and New Horizons."

Thriving in the Ever-Evolving Digital Landscape

In the fast-paced digital world, staying ahead of trends and evolving platforms is key to sustaining your pet's online influence. Embracing change and being open to experimenting with new content types and platforms can propel your pet's brand to new heights.

Examples and Tips for Keeping Up with Trends:

1. Engage in Influencer Communities: Join influencer communities or social media groups where content creators discuss trends, challenges, and best practices. Networking with peers can provide valuable insights and support.

2. Experiment with New Platforms: Explore emerging social media platforms to understand their potential for reaching a broader audience. Platforms like Clubhouse, TikTok, or Twitch may offer unique opportunities for pet influencers.

3. Adopt New Content Types: Stay open to trying different content formats, such as live streams, short-form videos, or interactive polls. Diversifying your content can keep your audience engaged and attract new followers.

4. Monitor Influential Accounts: Keep an eye on successful pet influencers or other content creators in your niche to identify trends and strategies that resonate with their audiences.

5. Stay Updated on Industry News: Regularly read industry blogs, watch webinars, and attend workshops focused on digital trends and social media marketing. These resources can provide valuable insights into the ever-changing landscape.

6. Data-Driven Decision Making: Use analytics and data from your pet's social media platforms to identify content that resonates with your audience. Analyze what performs well and adjust your content strategy accordingly.

Action Step:

1. Trend Research Time: Set aside dedicated time each week to research current digital trends and explore how they might align with your pet's brand.

2. Platform Exploration: Experiment with a new social media platform that you haven't used before. Create a presence and test different content types to see how your pet's audience responds.

3. Content Format Trial: Try incorporating a new content format into your pet's content plan, such as a live Q&A session, an interactive poll, or a behind-the-scenes video.

4. Industry Webinars or Workshops: Attend a webinar or workshop focused on social media trends and marketing strategies. Take notes and apply the insights to your pet's content strategy.

Remaining adaptable and embracing change is essential in the dynamic world of social media. By actively participating in influencer communities, experimenting with new platforms and content types, and staying informed about industry trends, you can ensure your pet continues to shine brightly in the digital spotlight.

32. Beyond the Screen: Exploring New Ventures

"From Viral Star to Real-World Success: Expanding Horizons."

Leveraging Fame into Exciting Opportunities

Your pet's online fame can open doors to a myriad of opportunities beyond the digital realm. As you explore new ventures, it's essential to identify your pet's unique strengths and how they can transition into successful real-world endeavors.

Examples and Tips for Transitioning to New Ventures:

1. Identify Unique Qualities: Analyze your pet's online presence and identify the traits or skills that set them apart. For example, if your pet is known for their charm and playful demeanor, they could become a brand ambassador for pet toys or accessories.

2. Networking and Collaboration: Connect with industry professionals, pet businesses, or other influencers to explore potential partnerships or collaborations. Working with established brands or personalities can amplify your pet's reach and influence.

3. Pet Product Line: Create a pet product line inspired by your pet's persona. It could include merchandise, pet accessories, or even a line of pet-friendly treats.

4. Pet Books or Merchandising: Consider creating a children's book series or comic strips featuring your pet's adventures. Merchandising opportunities like plush toys or collectibles could also be explored.

5. Charitable Initiatives: Leverage your pet's fame to support charitable causes or animal shelters. You can organize fundraisers or events to benefit the pet community.

6. Pet-Focused Events: Host pet-themed events or workshops in your local community or collaborate with pet businesses to promote pet care and well-being.

Action Step:

1. Strengths Assessment: List down your pet's unique traits, skills, or qualities that could translate well into real-world ventures.

2. Venture Brainstorming: Brainstorm three potential ventures outside of the digital space that align with your pet's brand and strengths. Consider how these ventures can provide value to your pet's audience and followers.

3. Reach Out and Collaborate: Begin reaching out to industry professionals, brands, or organizations that may be interested in collaborating with your pet on new ventures.

Your pet's online fame can act as a launching pad for exciting real-world opportunities. By identifying their strengths, networking with industry professionals, and exploring innovative ventures, you can continue to expand your pet's influence and impact in the pet-loving community.

33. A Lasting Paw Print: Preserving Your Pet's Impact

"Beyond the Digital Realm: Carving a Timeless Legacy."

Ensuring Your Pet's Impact Endures

While the internet is ever-changing, the impact your pet makes can extend far beyond the digital landscape. By creating meaningful content, engaging in charitable activities, and documenting your pet's journey, you can leave a lasting legacy that resonates with your pet's audience and the pet-loving community.

Examples and Tips for Leaving a Legacy:

1. Evergreen Content: Create evergreen content that remains relevant and valuable to your pet's audience even as trends and platforms evolve. Timeless content, such as pet care guides, training tips, or heartwarming stories, can continue to inspire and educate for years to come.

2. Charitable Activities: Dedicate time and effort to support charitable causes or animal advocacy aligned with your pet's values. Organize fundraisers, awareness campaigns, or events to benefit pets in need, leaving a positive impact on the pet community.

*3. Documentary or Memoir:*Consider creating a documentary or writing a memoir about your pet's journey as an influencer. Share behind-the-scenes stories, challenges, and the moments that shaped your pet's fame, inspiring others with your unique experience.

4. Memorializing Your Pet: If, unfortunately, your pet passes away, consider creating a memorial page or website where their impact and contributions are celebrated. Share cherished memories and invite others to share their experiences with your pet.

5. Collaboration with Charities: Partner with pet-related charities or rescue organizations to amplify your impact. Collaborate on projects, offer your pet's influence to raise awareness, or donate a portion of your pet's earnings to support their initiatives.

*6. Educational Initiatives:*Use your pet's influence to promote pet care, adoption, and responsible ownership. Create educational content or workshops that empower pet owners to provide the best care for their furry companions.

Action Step:

1. Select a Charitable Cause: Choose a charitable cause related to pets that aligns with your pet's values and passion. Research organizations or initiatives that address the cause you wish to support.

2. Plan a Campaign or Event: Develop a campaign or event that leverages your pet's influence to raise awareness or funds for the chosen cause. Involve your pet's audience and followers in the initiative to create a sense of community and shared impact.

3. Document Your Journey: Begin documenting your pet's journey as an influencer, capturing memorable moments, and reflecting on the lessons learned along the way. This documentation can serve as the foundation for potential future memoirs or documentaries.

Leaving a lasting legacy requires thoughtful consideration and a commitment to making a positive impact beyond the digital realm. By creating evergreen content, engaging in charitable activities, and documenting your pet's journey, your pet's influence can continue to resonate with others and inspire a love for pets for years to come.

34. Navigating the Heart's Journey: Facing the Inevitable

"Honoring the Memory and Celebrating the Journey."

Coping with the Loss of a Cherished Companion

The bond between a pet and their owner is profound and deeply personal. As pet influencers, this bond is also shared with a wider audience. Preparing for the inevitable loss of a pet is a delicate balance between personal grief and the shared sorrow of a community.

Examples and Tips for Handling Loss:

1. Social Media Hiatus: It's okay to take a break from social media to process your emotions and grieve privately. Inform your audience about your hiatus, so they understand and respect your need for space.

2. Celebrating Their Life: Share a heartfelt post or video that celebrates your pet's life, highlighting the joy, laughter, and memories they brought into the world. This can be therapeutic for you and provide closure for your audience.

3. Tribute Video or Photo Album: Create a tribute video or photo album that captures your pet's most cherished moments. This can serve as a lasting memory and a way for your audience to remember and celebrate your pet.

4. Memorial Space: Dedicate a space on your platform, such as a memorial page or a pinned post, where followers can share their memories, stories, or condolences.

5. Seek Support: Grieving the loss of a pet can be overwhelming. Consider joining support groups, seeking therapy, or connecting with others who have experienced a similar loss.

6. Charitable Acts: In memory of your pet, consider supporting a charitable cause or organization that aligns with your pet's values or passions. This can be a way to honor their legacy and make a positive impact.

Action Step:

1. Memory Keepsake: Begin creating a digital folder or scrapbook that captures your pet's most memorable moments. Include photos, videos, and notes that reflect their personality and the journey you've shared. This keepsake can serve as a comforting reminder of the love and joy they brought into your life.

2. Plan Ahead: While it's challenging to think about, consider drafting a post or message in advance that can be shared with your audience when the time comes. This can help ensure that you communicate in a way that feels right for you, without the pressure of crafting a message during a time of grief.

The loss of a pet is a profound experience, filled with a myriad of emotions. By preparing in advance, celebrating their life, and seeking support, you can navigate this challenging journey with grace and ensure that your pet's memory lives on, both in your heart and in the hearts of your audience.

35: Reflecting on the Journey

"Every tail wag, purr, chirp, or flutter captured and shared is a testament to the bond between pets and their humans."

As we come to the end of this handbook, it's essential to pause and reflect on the journey of pet influencing. It's not just about the viral moments, brand collaborations, or the number of followers. At its core, it's about celebrating the unique bond you share with your pet and the joy they bring into your life.

1. The Impact of Authenticity

In a digital age filled with filters and curated realities, authenticity stands out. Your pet, with their unfiltered emotions and genuine antics, has the power to connect with people on a profound level.

Cherish that authenticity, and let it be the guiding force behind your content.

2. The Responsibility of Influence

With influence comes responsibility. As your pet's primary advocate, it's your duty to ensure their well-being, both online and offline. From the brands you choose to collaborate with to the amount of time spent on content creation, always prioritize your pet's comfort and happiness.

3. Celebrating Milestones

Whether it's hitting a follower milestone, securing a dream collaboration, or simply capturing a perfect moment, celebrate the small victories. Each achievement is a step forward in your journey and a testament to the effort and love you've poured into your pet's online presence.

4. The Legacy of Love

Beyond the likes, comments, and shares, the true legacy of your pet's online journey is the love and happiness they've spread. For many of your followers, your content might be a bright spot in their day, a source of inspiration, or a reminder of the simple joys of life.

5. Looking Ahead

The world of pet influencing will continue to evolve, with new platforms, trends, and opportunities emerging. Stay adaptable, keep learning, and remember the core essence of why you started this journey: to share the love and joy of your pet with the world.

AFTERWORD

As we reach the end of this guide, it's essential to reflect on the journey we've embarked upon together. The world of pet influencing, as we've discovered, is as vast as it is vibrant. But beyond the strategies, tips, and techniques, there's a core truth that binds every pet influencer: a deep love and appreciation for their animal companion.

Making your pet internet famous is not just about the likes, shares, or brand collaborations. It's about sharing a piece of your world, your bond, and the countless heartwarming moments that come with pet ownership. It's about creating a space where others can find joy, solace, and inspiration in the antics and adventures of your furry, feathered, or finned friend.

However, with the spotlight comes responsibility. As you navigate the digital realm, always prioritize your pet's well-being and happiness. The internet may be fleeting, but the bond you share with your pet is timeless. Cherish it, nurture it, and let it be the guiding force behind every post, video, or story you share.

To everyone who has picked up this handbook, whether you're just starting out or are a seasoned pet influencer, thank you. Thank you for your passion, your dedication, and for sharing the magic of your pet with the world. The digital landscape is ever-evolving, but the love we hold for our pets remains a constant.

Here's to the next chapter of your pet's online journey. May it be filled with joy, discovery, and countless memorable moments.